This copy of
THE JOKE – A – DAY
FUN BOOK

belongs to

_____

THE JOKE-A-DAY FUN BOOK

Janet Rogers

Illustrated by Bob Nixon

Beaver Books

A Beaver Book
Published by Arrow Books Limited
62-65 Chandos Place, London WC2N 4NW

An imprint of Century Hutchinson Ltd

London Melbourne Sydney Auckland
Johannesburg and agencies throughout the world

First published 1986

Text © Victorama Ltd 1986
Illustrations © Century Hutchinson 1986

Set in Baskerville by JH Graphics Ltd, Reading

Made and printed in Great Britain
by Anchor Brendon Ltd, Tiptree, Essex

ISBN 0 09 941990 4

Introduction

Here it is at last – the Joke-a-Day Fun Book! Jolly jokes, ridiculous riddles, cheeky challenges, potty people, barmy books, wacky waiters, daffy doctors – all are here. There's something to make you laugh on every single day of the year. There are famous people's birthdays and notable dates, too, and there is your own personal space for each day, a space for you to fill with your Joke of the Day/Thought for the Day/a Record of your Friends' Birthdays. . . whatever you like.

JANUARY

January 1

The beginning of a new year is always an exciting time. It's a time for making resolutions and looking forward to the twelve months ahead. Do you know what my New Year's resolution is going to be? To make every day a Special Joke Day so that, whatever happens, this year will be full of chortles and chuckles, giggles and guffaws.

What's your resolution going to be?

Of course, if you were a caterpillar, you would know exactly what to do – you'd simply turn over a new leaf!

Your own space _____

_____

_____

January 2

Don't be too ambitious with your New Year's resolution, like Mad Professor Pikestaff with his crazy cross-breeding.

He has decided to cross a woodpecker with a carrier pigeon. That way he hopes to end up with a bird which knocks before delivering its message!

Your own space _____

_____

_____

January 3

A New Year's Knock-knock
Knock, knock.
Who's there?
Hosanna.
Hosanna who?
Hosanna Claus got down our tiny chimney at Christmas, I will never know.

Your own space _____

_____

_____

January 4

Ridiculous Riddle
What sort of bird is always out of breath?
A puffin.

Your own space _____

_____

_____

January 5

Potty People
What do you call a girl with a log fire on her head?
Anita.

Your own space _____

_____

_____

January 6

How about a Cheeky Challenge?
Persuade a friend to stand with his or her left side
against a wall, so that both his or her left foot and
cheek touch the wall, then bet them they can't lift up
their right foot. You will win because it can't be done,
because in order to lift the right foot the friend will
first have to move slightly to the right, which will not
be possible with the left foot and cheek touching the
wall.

Your own space _____

_____

_____

January 7

If two's company, and three's a crowd, what's four and five?
Nine, of course.

Your own space _____

_____

_____

January 8

The pop star David Bowie was born on 8 January 1947. He's sold millions of records all over the world. Perhaps you've got records like 'Space Oddity', 'Heroes', and 'Let's Dance' in your collection.

Talking of dancing, have you read about the new dance craze that's sweeping America? It's called the Lift. It's very easy to learn, though there is a slight problem – it's got no steps!

Your own space _____

_____

_____

January 9

Have you read any good books lately? I can certainly recommend these for a good laugh:

A Lucky Escape	by Justin Time
Journey to the South Pole	by Anne Tarctic
All Lit Up	by Alec Tricity
The Highton Grange Murders	by Hugh Dunnit

Your own space _____

_____

_____

January 10

Try to get your tongue around this Mighty Mouthful!

Shares in Sarah Sharer's sea-shell shop shot up so sharply last summer, she soon had six skyscrapers standing side by side, shimmering on the sandy seashore.

Your own space _____

_____

_____

January 11

Geography Question
Are there any fat people in Finland?

Your own space _____

_____

_____

January 12

Medical Madness
PATIENT: *Doctor, Doctor, I keep thinking I'm a soft drink!*
DOCTOR: I told you not to play squash.

Your own space _____

_____

_____

January 13

A Foreign Newsflash has just come in from Paris:
  'A fully-clothed man jumped from the Pont Neuf
  into the river below this morning. The police were

unable to discover a reason for the man's strange behaviour, and have declared him in Seine.'

Your own space _____

_____

_____

January 14

An Ancient Riddle
What did Noah say when the Heavens opened and rain flooded the earth?
ARK!

Your own space _____

_____

_____

January 15

My sister can't stand graffiti – in fact she doesn't like any foreign food! She certainly wouldn't be able to stomach this lot:

DOWN WITH GRAVITY
Exits are on the way out
JAMES BOND RULES 007
Nostalgia isn't what it used to be

Your own space _____

_____

_____

January 16

An Amazing Animal Fact
Do you know why vultures eat raw meat?
Because they can't cook!

Your own space _____

_____

_____

January 17

Sign in a stationer's window
Calendars and diaries. All with one year's guarantee.

Your own space _____

_____

_____

January 18

January's Loopy Limerick
A young man called Archibald Rose
Had a rather large mole on his nose.
When it was removed
His appearance improved,
But his glasses slipped down to his toes.

Your own space _____

_____

_____

January 19

Notice in newsagent's window
Woman wants washing and cleaning two days a week.

Your own space _we had Games they were goo we one 4-0 in Hockey I S them all._

January 20

Little Lester Lasso was furious when he noticed that his horse had been tampered with while he was away. He burst into the crowded saloon and yelled at the top of his voice: 'Okay, which of you low-down varmints painted my horse red?'

A huge cowboy walked forward from the back of the room and picked Lester up by his lapels. 'It was me, Shorty,' he growled. 'What about it?'

'Oh, nothing, er, nothing at all,' stammered Lester, shaking all over. 'I just wanted to know if it needed another coat. . .!'

Your own space _Today was good we had craft and I watched East Ender_

January 21

If you have an umpire in tennis and a referee in football, what do you have in bowls?
Goldfish.

Your own space _Today was pe and we had no swimming._

January 22

Wise Saying of the Month
No one's legs are so short they won't reach the ground.

Your own space _Today we had Miss briggs for music you had to sing your name_

January 23

JOANNA: *Miss, whose last words were, 'Is it over yet?'*
TEACHER: I don't know, Joanna. Please tell me.
JOANNA: *Mine!*

Your own space _Today we won in football and we had art_

January 24

A Culinary Cackle
CUSTOMER: *Why is my food so dirty and mushed up?*
WAITER: You did ask me to step on it.

Your own space _Today Lisa went to cross cuntry she came 78 out of cbout 150._

January 25

Not many people know that today is National Elk
Day in Mongolia. A famous Mongolian recipe that
has come down to me through the ages requires only
two ingredients–an elk and a pound of strawberries.
The result is a delicious STRAWBERRY MOOSE!

Your own space _Today cris_
rogers came to stay
and one Saturday we watched
the pantomind

January 26

A January Jingle
A little birdie flying by,
Dropped a message from the sky.
A passing farmer wiped his eye;
Said he: 'I'm glad that cows can't fly.'

Your own space _Today we_
have got fotball
the Score was 2·0 we
won peyul Scored 2 I set
_up_

January 27

Fifty pedigree dogs were stolen from Cruft's Dog
Show yesterday. Police say they have no leads.

Your own space _Today we_
had craft we
cur doing puppeti

January 28

Are you a practical joker?

If so, here's one to add to your collection:

Get a friend to sit on a straight-backed chair which has no arms. Their feet must be flat on the floor and their back resting on the back of the chair. Now challenge them to stand up, without moving their feet or back from the positions they are in. It can't be done, and if they remain sitting in that position they will be sitting in the chair forever!

Your own space _Today we have Swimming it was good_

January 29

What's got six legs and can fly long distances?
Three swallows.

Your own space _Today we have music and Tables, we had h:ss rigg_

January 30

Sign in large hotel
If there is a fire, please do your best to alarm the Hall Porter.

Your own space _Today we had out we out dong a collarge_

19

January 31

Two newly-married women were discussing their mothers-in-law. One said, 'I wouldn't say Bert's mother was mean, but she keeps a fork in the sugar bowl.'

Your own space _today I have nearly finshed the Sheffield wednsday page_

February 1

Let's start the month with another of those Potty People!
What do you call a woman with a frog on her head?
Lily!

Your own space _Today I was_
at peters and I baught
6 packets of stickers

February 2

Here's some graffiti spotted on a nearby wall:
I LOVE GRILS
(*Under which someone else has written:*)
You silly fool, you mean I LOVE GIRLS
(*And yet another person has added:*)
WHAT'S WRONG WITH US GRILS!

Your own space _Today i had_
hoky we wen
4-0 i scored 4

February 3

Why did the busy bee buzz past with its back legs crossed?
Because it was desperately searching for a BP station.

Your own space Today we have craft Miss clence wasn't there.

February 4

Notice in kitchen
Anyone making use of the coffee cups, please wash
them thoroughly before leaving, and then stand
upside down in the sink.

Your own space Today we didn't have swimming Because Miss clence wasn't there

February 5

FATHER: *What's the matter, Son?*
SON: I've lost the dog.
FATHER: Don't worry, we'll put a notice in the
    paper – LOST DOG, PLEASE RETURN.
SON: But Dad, I don't think Rex can read.

Your own space Today Miss riggs did Music we craked up

February 6

Hey Diddle Diddle, Here Comes a Riddle!
When is it correct to say 'I is'?
When you say: 'I is the letter after H.'

Your own space _tomorow I_
am going to rosser
party.

February 7

If your teacher ever asks you to define the meaning of
a particular word, always remember that there are
two possibilities – the correct definition and the
DAFT DEFINITION. Take these examples:

FOUL LANGUAGE	Cursing hens
ILLEGAL	A bird that is unwell
UNIT	A term of abuse
YANK	An American dentist

Your own space _Today I went_
to rosses party we
watched the Gremlins

February 8

One-liner of the Month
My father used to work in the biscuit factory down
the road, but he had to leave–the job was driving him
crackers!

Your own space _Today was boring my mum went barmy on my homework_

February 9

If you're one of those people who can't wait for the weekend to arrive, you would probably enjoy the book I've just been reading. It's called *The End of the Week* by Gladys Friday.

Your own space _Today I got a love letter of my girlfriend (patty)_

February 10

Here's another Cheeky Challenge to try on your friends!
Challenge them to knock a glass of water on the floor without spilling any. No one will believe it can be done, but it can. All you have to do is place the glass of water on the floor, and give it a couple of gentle taps. The glass has been knocked on the floor, but there's no water to mop up!

Your own space _____

_____

_____

February 11

When your teacher next asks you to name three collective nouns, give the whole class a shock and say, 'The hoover, the dustbin, and the dustpan!'

Your own space _____

_____

_____

February 12

Wise Saying of the Month
Anything is possible if you don't know what you're talking about.

Your own space _____

_____

_____

February 13

Come in, February's Knock-knock!
Knock, knock.
Who's there?
Felix.
Felix who?
Felix my lolly, I'll kick him!

Your own space _____

_____

_____

February 14

Today is Valentine's Day, the day for lovers. Which reminds me of a romantic conversation I overheard in a restaurant the other day:

My girlfriend's a twin.
How can you tell them apart?
Her brother's got a beard.

Your own space _today Ian going to slimbridge with Miss brown_

February 15

Did you hear about the cowboy with paper trousers?
The sheriff put him in jail for rustling!

Your own space _Today Im going to bens party._

February 16

PATIENT: *Doctor, Doctor, I keep thinking I'm a pound note.*
DOCTOR: *Well, go and buy some sweets—the change will do you good.*

Your own space _____

_____

_____

February 17

This crazy advertisement appeared recently in an Indian newspaper:

FOR SALE–Fully-grown lion. House-trained and affectionate, it will happily eat flesh from your hand.

Your own space _____

_____

_____

February 18

NEWSFLASH. . . .
'The police are looking for a man with one ear called Welsh Len. They have not yet released the name of the other ear.'

Your own space _____

_____

_____

February 19

Thought for the Month
If your cat swallows a pound coin, does it mean you've got some money in the kitty?

Your own space _____

_____

_____

February 20

Q. *What's the similarity between getting up at six in the morning and a pig's tail?*

A. Both of them are twirly (too early).

Your own space _____

_____

_____

February 21

Waiter, Waiter, what do you call this?
Cottage pie, Sir.
Well, I've just cut my mouth on a window.

Your own space _____

_____

_____

February 22

Be a devil for the day and play this practical joke on someone. Telephone a friend and carry out the following conversation:

YOU: *Is Alice Wall there, please?*
VICTIM: No.
YOU: *Is Mr Wall there then, please?*
VICTIM: No. Are you sure you've got the right number?
VICTIM: *Are there any Walls there at all?*

VICTIM: No, there aren't.
YOU: *Gosh, it must be awfully cold!*

Your own space _____

_____

_____

February 23

On 23 February 1955, the pop star Howard Jones was born. Did you know that Howard Jones never eats meat and is a vegetarian?

I wonder whether he knows any cannibals who are vegetarians – they'd only be allowed to eat Swedes!

Your own space _____

_____

_____

February 24
February's Loopy Limerick
There was a young man from Devizes
Whose eyes were of different sizes.
The one that was small
Was no use at all,
But the big one won several prizes.

Your own space _____

_____

_____

February 25

If you think you're good a tongue-twisters, try this
one for size:

Six spy ships slid slowly southwards over the sea.
(And now repeat it quickly three times!)

Your own space _____

_____

_____

February 26

Do you know anyone whose name suits their job
particularly well?

There's a man in Birmingham called Walter Wall.
He's a carpet salesman!

Your own space _____

_____

_____

February 27

What do you get if you cross a flea with a rabbit?
Bugs Bunny.

Your own space _____

_____

_____

February 28

1ST VOICE: *Mummy, Mummy, I don't want to go to school today.*

2ND VOICE: Don't be silly, dear, you've got to go.

1ST VOICE: *Why?*

2ND VOICE: For a start, your're sixty years old, and secondly you're the Headmaster!

Your own space _____

_____

_____

February 29 (Leap Years Only)

The Amazing World of Nature
Pelicans are very expensive animals to feed.
Why?—because they have such large bills!

Your own space _____

_____

_____

MARCH

March 1

March 1st is St David's Day, the day when all good Welshmen and women stick a daffodil in their buttonholes.

To celebrate today, why not sample a book by a Welsh author. For starters, you might like to dip into that best-selling book, *Slimming is Fun* by Dai Ting!

Your own space _____

_____

_____

March 2

Who makes suits and eats spinach?
Popeye the Tailorman.

Your own space _____

_____

_____

March 3

A Mysterious Verse
What is the beginning of Eternity,
The End of Time and Space,
The beginning of every End,
And the end of every Race?

The letter 'E', of course.

Your own space _____

_____

_____

March 4

Rock'n'roller Shakin' Stevens was born on 4 March 1948. He's had lots of hit songs, but how many of you know that his most famous song is based on his date of birth? It's a rhythmic little ditty called 'March Forth'.

Your own space _____

_____

_____

March 5

A March Shaggy Dog Story
The football team Plymouth Argyle had lost their last thirty matches, when their manager decided to buy them a new lucky mascot. Everyone was a little shocked when he turned up the next day with a toy demon, but it seemed to do the trick. They beat

Liverpool 10–0 in the FA Cup, and went on to remain unbeaten for the rest of the season. When the manager was asked by a reporter why he had chosen a toy demon as the club's mascot, he replied: 'Demons are Argyle's best friend.'

Your own space _____

_____

_____

March 6

A Rib-tickling Riddle
How do ghost-hunters keep fit?
By exorcizing regularly.

Your own space _____

_____

_____

March 7

The next time your Science teacher tries to catch you out by asking the meaning of the word 'bacteria', don't hesitate . . . just tell her the truth. A bacteria is the rear entrance of a cafeteria!

Your own space _____

_____

_____

March 8

Monster Fun!

Why are monsters so forgetful?
Because everything you tell them goes in one ear and out the others.

Your own space _Dads birthday_

March 9

Did you hear about the plastic surgeon who just died?
He sat on a radiator and made a complete pool of himself.

Your own space

March 10

More Potty People (just like Pretty Patrick Peterson)

What do you call a man with a spade on his head?
Doug!

Your own space

March 11

Potty People (cont.)
What do you call a man who hasn't got a spade on his head?
Douglas!

Your own space _____

_____

_____

March 12

Today's Tricky Tongue-twister
Pretty Patrick Peterson prayed that people picked
his picture from the parade of portraits perched
perilously on the podium.

When no one picked his picture, Pretty Patrick
Peterson pestered the patron of the Picture Palace for
his promised payment. (PHEW!)

Your own space _____

_____

_____

March 13

Medical Madness
PATIENT: *Doctor, Doctor, I've only got 59 seconds to live.*
   Can you help me?
DOCTOR: Come and sit down over here for a minute.

Your own space _____

_____

_____

March 14

Whacky Wisdom
No matter where you go, there you are.

Your own space _____

_____

_____

March 15

March's Loopy Limerick
There was an old man called Debrett,
Whose great joy in life was to bet.
All his resources
Went on the horses,
That's why he was always in debt.

Your own space _____

_____

_____

March 16

It All Adds Up!
What's five Q and five Q?
Ten Q.
You're welcome.

Your own space _____

_____

_____

March 17

**Let the Irish rejoice, for today is St Patrick's Day
– hip, hip, hooray! Here's a special Irish Knock-
knock:**
Knock, knock.
Who's there?
Eamon.
Eamon who?
Eamon a great mood – it's St Patrick's Day.

Your own space _____

_____

_____

March 18

NEWS ... NEWS ... NEWS
A set of traffic lights was stolen from the High Street
today. A police spokesperson commented, 'Some
thieves will stop at nothing.'

Your own space _____

_____

_____

March 19

Cheeky Challenge of the Month
Try out this challenge on a friend – you are bound to
win. Simply bet your friend that you can jump across
the road. Your friend will probably try to put you off,
for it sounds as if it might be a dangerous thing to do,
and he or she certainly won't believe you can do it.

It's very easy to do though. Simply cross the road, and when you are on the other side, jump up in the air. You will have jumped across the road!

Your own space _____

_____

_____

March 20

What does Princess Diana say to Prince William when he does something naughty?
If you don't stop it, I'll crown you!

Your own space _____

_____

_____

March 21

The prize for the funniest book of the month has to go to that hilarious story of one woman's ups and downs: *I Blushed All Day* by Lucy Lastic.

Your own space _____

_____

_____

March 22

Do you know anyone you'd like to play a really hilarious practical joke on today? Here's one to try.

Challenge a friend to a whistling contest. But before he or she starts, persuade him or her to suck a piece of lemon. If your friend refuses to do this, you suck it standing close to them when they try to whistle. Either way they should find it impossible to whistle at all, because the bitter taste of the lemon, either real or imagined, makes it impossible to get the lips to form the right shape.

Your own space _____

_____

_____

March 23

How many conkers grow on the average oak tree?
None. Conkers don't grow on oak trees!

Your own space _____

_____

_____

March 24

'Where have you been, Charlie?' demanded the Scoutmaster angrily.

'I'm sorry,' said Charlie, 'but as we walked through that field of cows my beret blew off and I had to try on twenty before I found it.'

Your own space _____

_____

_____

March 25

PATIENT: *I'm still not getting much sleep at nights.*
DOCTOR: Do you mean you haven't been taking those sleeping pills I gave you?
PATIENT: *No. They looked so happy and peaceful in the bottle, I didn't have the heart to wake them up.*

Your own space _____

_____

_____

March 26

MUSIC MISTRESS: *You have a fine, powerful voice, Nina.*
NINA: I have to have, Miss.
MUSIC MISTRESS: *Why's that?*
NINA: Because in our house there's no lock on the lavatory door.

Your own space _____

_____

_____

March 27

The Wonderful World of Nature
Aren't dolphins clever animals? Within weeks of being captured, they are able to train a human being to stand at the side of the pool, and throw them endless supplies of fish.

Your own space _____

_____

_____

March 28

MUSIC MISTRESS: *You have a fine, powerful voice, Nina.*
NINA: I have to have, Miss.
MUSIC MISTRESS: *Why's that?*
NINA: Because in our house there's no lock on the lavatory door.

Your own space _____

_____

_____

March 29

What circles the lampshade at 200 kilometres per hour?
Stirling Moth.

Your own space _____

_____

_____

March 30

A man took his pet alsatian to see *The Jungle Book* at the local cinema. The usherette was amazed when she noticed the dog laughing and giggling throughout the film. The alsatian even stood up on its hind legs at the end and applauded.

As they were leaving, the usherette walked over to the man and said: 'I can't believe it. Your dog really enjoyed the film.'

'Neither can I,' replied the man. 'He hated the book.'

Your own space _____

_____

_____

March 31

A ghost teacher was showing her young pupils how to walk through walls. 'Did you all follow that?' she asked. 'If not, I'll go through it again.'

Your own space _____

_____

_____

APRIL

April 1

Shhh! It's April Fool's Day today. Keep it quiet – you don't want everyone in on the joke. Plan out your April Fool in advance, choose your victim, then, if all goes well, by all means shout about it afterwards. An April Fool that always works well is the famous 'Quick Dressing Routine'.

Get up earlier than usual this morning, put your normal clothes on, and then get straight back into bed. Ignore any calls from your family to get up at the usual time, and pretend to be fast asleep. When someone complains that you're late getting up, assure them that you could be up and dressed in a matter of seconds rather than minutes if you wanted. If anyone questions this statement, bet them a pound that you can do it. Ask them to step outside, and emerge from your room a few seconds later fully dressed. It's always nice to start the month a pound richer, don't you agree?

Your own space _____

_____

_____

April 2

Here's a Knock-knock that can be particularly useful when you want to get your hands on some friend's chocolate:
Knock, knock.
Who's there?
Sharon.
Sharon who?
Sharon share alike – please may I have some chocolate?

Your own space _____

_____

_____

April 3

1ST SECRETARY: *Do you ever file your nails?*
2ND SECRETARY: No, I usually just throw them away.

Your own space _____

_____

_____

April 4

Wise Saying of the Month
If at first you don't succeed . . . you're just like 99 per cent of the rest of the population.

Your own space _____

_____

_____

April 5

Medical Madness

PATIENT: *Doctor, Doctor, I've got a terrible fever. I'm literally boiling.*

DOCTOR: Simmer down a little, Sir.

Your own space _____

_____

_____

April 6

Thought for the Day
Is the sport of fishing so popular because it's easy to get hooked on?

Your own space _____

_____

_____

April 7

Schoolroom Capers

TEACHER: *What is a panther, Terry?*

TERRY: (*hesitating*) Er . . . er . . . is it a person who panths, Miss?

Your own space _____

_____

_____

April 8

How About a Really Silly Game?

First, spread several sheets of newspaper over the floor, so that you don't make any mess. Then fill a large, shallow bowl with flour so that it's about half full. Get hold of some buttons and give them a wash, then drop them into the bowl. Once the buttons are well and truly buried, invite the first player to pick a penny out using ONLY THEIR TEETH! You should have a few flour-spattered faces by the end of this game.

Your own space _____

_____

_____

April 9

Why are you so angry?
It's all the rage.

Your own space _____

_____

_____

April 10

What are you doing with all those packets of steel wool?
I'm going to knit a car.

Your own space _____

_____

_____

April 11

Hey Diddle Diddle, Here comes a Riddle!

Q. *Why is 'B' such a hot letter?*
A. Because it can make oil boil.

Your own space _____

_____

_____

April 12

Sign in a chemist's shop
Feeling tired and run down? Try our Super-Vitamin
Tonic. We guarantee you'll never get better.

Your own space _____

_____

_____

April 13

April's Loopy Limerick
There once was a man from Ealing
Who had this very strange feeling,
That if he sat down
And put on a crown,
Gold would fall through the ceiling.

Your own space _____

_____

_____

April 14

DINER: *Waiter, Waiter, there's a fly in my soup.*
WAITER: Thank you for pointing it out, Sir. I'll call the RSPCA immediately.

Your own space _____

_____

_____

April 15

1ST WOMAN: *We've just had an Egyptian doorbell installed.*
2ND WOMAN: How does that work?
1ST WOMAN: *You just toot and come in.*

Your own space _____

_____

_____

April 16

An April Shaggy Dog Story
Stan persuaded one of his friends to buy twenty raffle tickets from him the day before the draw was due to be held. A few days later the two men met up again, and Stan was asked how the draw went.

  'I won first prize,' replied Stan. 'Wasn't I lucky?'
  'And who won the second prize?' asked his friend.
  'My wife did. Wasn't she lucky?'
  'She certainly was. And who won third prize?'
  'My daughter won third prize,' said Stan. 'Wasn't

she lucky? By the way, you haven't paid me yet for those twenty tickets you bought.'

'So I haven't,' said his friend. 'Aren't I lucky?'

Your own space _____

_____

_____

April 17

A History Lesson

Q. *Do you know what the Tsar of Russia used to call his children?*

A. Tsardines.

Your own space _____

_____

_____

April 18

More Daft Definitions

ADDRESS   What girls wear.
KIDNAP   A child having a rest.
ELEPHANT   A very large ant.
ICE CREAM   What do you do if you're angry.

Your own space _____

_____

_____

April 19

Crazy Graffiti
I'D GIVE MY RIGHT ARM TO BE
AMBIDEXTROUS!

Your own space _____

_____

_____

April 20

SARAH: A millionaire has really got what it takes.
EMMA: He certainly has. A million pounds to be
  precise!

Your own space _____

_____

_____

April 21

Books for Bird-brains
Show Jumping for Beginners   by Jim Carner
The Suicide   by Willie Jump
A Walk in the Park   by Theresa Greene

Your own space _____

_____

_____

April 22

April's One-liner
My brother is a light eater. As soon as it's light, he
starts eating!

Your own space _____

_____

_____

April 23

Today is St George's Day in memory of the brave
knight who slew the dragon. But I wonder if even
St George could have got his tongue round this
treacherous twister:

    Dumper the dastardly dragon dragged the
    dauntless damsel into his dark dungeon. When
    dapper Dick the dashing Duke saw the damsel in
    distress, he drove the dragon out of the dungeon.
    He drew his dagger and dug it into the dragon's
    side. The dragon died!

Your own space _____

_____

_____

April 24

Just a Thought
Are small judges just little things sent to try us?

Your own space _____

_____

_____

April 25

WOMAN: *Do you sell horses, meat?*
BUTCHER: Only if they are accompanied by their
  owners.

Your own space _____

_____

_____

April 26

At Cross Purposes?
What do you get if you cross a zebra and a monkey?
A zebkey!

Your own space _____

_____

_____

April 27

A man standing at a bus stop was passing the time by
eating some fish and chips. Next to him was a lady
with a dog, which kept jumping up at the man to try
and steal his supper.

  'Do you mind if I throw him a bit?' asked the man.
  'Not at all,' replied the lady.

  Whereupon the man picked up the dog and threw
him over a wall.

Your own space _____

_____

_____

April 28

Have you heard about the television addict who placed a mirror on top of the telly so he could see his wife from time to time?

Your own space _____

_____

_____

April 29

Knock, knock.
Who's there?
Arthur.
Arthur who?
Arthur 29 days in April? Or is it 30 . . . ?

Your own space _____

_____

_____

April 30
Let's finish April off with some of those Potty People!
What do you call an Irishman with two panes of glass on his head?
Paddy O'Doors (patio doors)!

Your own space _____

_____

_____

May 1

May is, of course, the shortest month of the year.
Why?
Because it's only got three letters!

Your own space _____

_____

_____

May 2

You may not realize it, but today is National Dog
Walking Day in Hong Kong – which reminds me of a
joke.
Q.   What do you get if you cross a terrier with a
     vegetable?
A.   A Jack Brussel.

Your own space _____

_____

_____

May 3

Money Matters

There's only one certain way of making your pocket money go further – post it to Australia.

Your own space _____

_____

_____

May 4

A man rushed into a pet shop and gasped, 'Let me have a mousetrap as quickly as possible, I've got a train to catch.'

The assistant looked surprised. 'I'm terribly sorry, Sir,' she replied. 'We haven't got any as big as that.'

Your own space _____

_____

_____

May 5

Hey Diddle Diddle, Here Comes a Riddle:

Q. *Why did it take four Boy Scouts to help one old lady across the road?*

A. Because she wanted to stay where she was!

Your own space _____

_____

_____

May 6

Try this trick on a friend. Suggest a game of cowboys and Indians, and say to your friend that you bet you can turn her/him into an Indian. The friend is bound to ask, 'How?' Whereupon you retort, 'See, I've started already!'

Your own space _____

_____

_____

May 7

Paddy and Mick saw a sign in a Dublin post office that said, 'Tree fellers wanted'. Mick said to Paddy, 'Do you think we could apply, seeing there's only two of us?'

Your own space _____

_____

_____

May 8

The Return of the Potty People!
What do you call a man with a number plate on his head?
Reg!

Your own space _____

_____

_____

May 9

Just a Thought
Do battery hens lay electric eggs?

Your own space _____

_____

_____

May 10

Peter couldn't swim. He fell in the river and was
floundering around desperately when his friend
called out, 'If you don't come up for the third time,
can I have your train set?'

Your own space _____

_____

_____

May 11

May's Loopy Limerick
There was an old lady from Leeds
Who swallowed a packet of seeds.
By the end of that hour
Her face was a flower,
And her head was all covered in weeds.

Your own space _____

_____

_____

May 12

NEWS ... NEWS ... NEWS
'A young lady dashed from the crowd and kissed
Prince Charles outside Buckingham Palace today.
He immediately turned into a frog.'

Your own space _____

_____

_____

May 13

Boxing News
MANAGER: *My new heavyweight is called 'Nuclear' Neil
   Clark.*
REPORTER: Why do you call him that?
MANAGER: *Because he's got guided muscles.*

Your own space _____

_____

_____

May 14

Ancient Wisdom
Keep Smiling – it makes everyone wonder what
you've been up to!

Your own space _____

_____

_____

May 15

The headmaster at our local school certainly doesn't believe in being soft with the children. He's already caned twelve children in his first week. I suppose I shouldn't be too surprised – he's an ex-army officer called Corporal Punishment.

Your own space _____

_____

_____

May 16

Police Warning
People are advised not to try to drink and drive. You're sure to spill some of it if you do.

Your own space _Lisas birthday_

_____

_____

May 17

Game for a Laugh?
People's feet tell you a lot about their personality, my grandmother used to say. Why don't you put her idea to the test, and invite your friends to play 'Fit the Foot'?

Split your group of friends into two teams. Get the first team to lie on the floor with a sheet covering everything but their bare feet. Then invite the other team to write down on a piece of paper which feet belong to which person.

Once that's been done, it's the second team's turn to bare their feet, and the first team's turn to guess who the feet belong to. (By the way, I'd advise you to make sure everybody washes their feet before you start!)

Your own space _Karens birthday_

_____

_____

May 18

Is it possible for a man with a large moustache to eat soup politely?
Yes, but it's a big strain.

Your own space _____

_____

_____

May 19

Medical Madness
PATIENT: Doctor, Doctor, every time I lift my arm up above my head, I get a terrible pain in my side.
DOCTOR: Well, don't do it then.

Your own space _____

_____

_____

May 20

A Short Poem
Po.

Your own space _____
_____
_____

May 21

A Musical Tip
I always say that the best way to reach the high notes
when singing is to stand on a table!

Your own space _____
_____
_____

May 22

Graffiti behind the bicycle shed:
George Sandelbury has got big ears!
(*Underneath which someone has written*:)
AND HE WON'T GIVE HIM BACK UNTIL
NODDY PAYS THE RANSOM.

Your own space _____
_____
_____

May 23

Q. *When does Friday come before Thursday?*
A. In a dictionary.

Your own space _____

_____

_____

May 24

May's Mighty Mouthful
My mother Mrs Marsh made me mountainous
mouthfuls of marvellous mushy mash.

Your own space _____

_____

_____

May 25

Books to read this month
The Ship is Sinking   by Mandy Pumps
Cookery made Simple   by Egon Toast
The World of Fashion   by Luke Good
How to Stop Drinking   by Alf Measures

Your own space _____

_____

_____

May 26

Food for Thought
Do fishermen make their nets by sewing hundreds of little holes together?

Your own space ———————————

———————————————————————

———————————————————————

May 27

Riddle-Tee-Hee!
Q.   Why was the insect chucked out of the park?
A.   Because it was a litterbug!

Your own space ———————————

———————————————————————

———————————————————————

May 28

ANGRY COMMUTER: *Excuse me, I've been waiting for ages.*
   How long will the next bus be?
INSPECTOR: About ten metres as usual, Sir.

Your own space ———————————

———————————————————————

———————————————————————

May 29

DINER: *Waiter, Waiter, this steak tastes funny.*
WAITER: So why don't you laugh?

Your own space _____

_____

_____

May 30

What do the police in Hawaii say when they see someone acting suspiciously?
Aloha, Aloha, Aloha, what's going on here then?

Your own space _____

_____

_____

May 31

LATE NEWSFLASH
'Doctors today warned against people trying to write on an empty stomach. They advise using paper instead.'

Your own space _____

_____

_____

JUNE

June 1

Medical Madness

DOCTOR: *I'm afraid that my tests show that you need to wear glasses.*

PATIENT: But, Doctor, I already do wear glasses.

DOCTOR: *In that case, I need some glasses!*

Your own space _____

_____

_____

June 2

A Silly Poem
Microbes
Adam
Had 'em.

Your own space _____

_____

_____

June 3

Q. *Why did the gerbil cross the road?*
A. Because it was tied to the leg of the chicken.

Your own space _____

_____

_____

June 4

TEACHER: *Timmy, what exactly are engineers?*
TIMMY: The things engines hear with, Sir.

Your own space _____

_____

_____

June 5

Just a Thought
If you had six bottles of lemonade, would you be able
to start a pop group?

Your own space _____

_____

_____

June 6

A Shaggy Dog Story
An enormous lion was strutting proudly through the
jungle one day, when he came across a zebra.

'Zebra,' he shouted, 'who is the King of the Jungle?'

'You are, of course,' replied the zebra timidly. A little further on, the lion saw a monkey.

'Monkey,' he roared, 'who is the King of the Jungle?'

'You are, Mr Lion,' said the monkey. 'No question.' A few minutes later the lion met an elephant.

'Elephant,' growled the lion, baring his teeth, 'who is the King of the Jungle?'

Suddenly the elephant picked the lion up with his trunk and threw him against a tree. He then swung him around three times in a circle, and hurled him into the nearest lake.

'All right,' grumbled the miserable, battered old lion. 'Just because you don't know the answer, there's no need to get cross.'

Your own space _____

_____

_____

June 7

Riddle-Tee-Hee!
What's brown and comes steaming out of Cowes?
The Isle of Wight ferry.

Your own space _____

_____

_____

June 8

What's the Italian for a helping of pie?
A pizza pie!

Your own space _____

_____

_____

June 9

Today is Vampire Memorial Day in Transylvania, the day when the inhabitants remember one of their most famous citizens – Count Dracula.

It's surprising that anyone wants to remember the ghoulish Count. After all, he was a bit of a pain in the neck!

Your own space _____

_____

_____

June 10

Daft Definitions
What's the definition of pointlessness?
Two bald men fighting over a comb.

Your own space _____

_____

_____

June 11

MOTHER: *Helen, answer the door, will you?*
HELEN: I can't, I didn't hear the question.

Your own space _____

_____

_____

June 12

Why was the Irishman buried on the right side of the hill?
Because he was dead.

Your own space _____

_____

_____

June 13

One-liner of the Month
Ed is so clever, it's not jokes he tells but wisecracks!

Your own space _____

_____

_____

June 14

Boy George was born on 14 June 1961. Which
reminds me of that great joke:

What do you get if you cross Boy George with a bird of prey?
Vulture Club!

Your own space _____

_____

_____

June 15

NEWS ... NEWS ... NEWS
'Two prisoners escaped from Dartmoor Prison early
this morning. One of the men is around 2 metres tall,
while his friend is just over a metre. The police are
searching high and low.'

Your own space _____

_____

_____

June 16

June's Mighty Mouthful
When Master Mather missed the maths master's
messages, the maths master made Master Mather
miss the match.

Your own space _____

_____

_____

June 17

Advertisement in the local paper
FOR SALE – 2KG BAGS OF SOIL. DIRT
CHEAP.

Your own space _____

_____

_____

June 18

Wise Saying of the Month
If the shoe fits, it's ugly.

Your own space _____

_____

_____

June 19

PATIENT: *Doctor, Doctor, I keep thinking I'm a bar of soap.*
DOCTOR: That's life, boy.

Your own space _____

_____

_____

June 20

Book of the Month
It Won't Take Long by Chester Minute

Your own space _____

_____

_____

June 21

Game for a Laugh?

This game will really test your powers of
concentration. How long do you think you can keep a
straight face while all around you are losing theirs?

Sit in a chair in the middle of the room, and ask
your friends to do all they can to make you laugh in
the space of just a minute (or 'Chester Minute'!).
They can tell jokes, make funny faces, and giggle as
much as they like. The only thing they're not allowed
to do is touch you.

Once you've had your go, let someone else take the
hot seat. I warn you it's not as easy as it looks.

Your own space _____

_____

_____

June 22

FRED: *Have you been invited to George's party?*
TOM: Yes, but I can't go. The invitation says 'Five to
Eight', and I was nine last month.

Your own space _____

_____

_____

June 23

Just a Thought
If you put cement in your tea, would you end up with a stiff drink?

Your own space _____

_____

_____

June 24

At Cross Purposes!
What do you get if you cross peanut butter with Bryan Robson?
A footballer that sticks to the roof of your mouth.

Your own space _____

_____

_____

June 25

MAN: *I'm terribly sorry, Madam. I've just run over your cat. Can I replace it for you?*
WOMAN: That's very kind, but I don't think you'd fit on my lap.

Your own space _____

_____

_____

June 26

More Potty People

What do you call a Cockney girl with a plate of bacon and eggs on her head?
Caff!

Your own space _____

_____

_____

June 27

Q. *How do you get down off a giraffe?*
A. You don't. You get down off a swan!

Your own space _____

_____

_____

June 28

SCIENCE TEACHER: *Can you name a shooting star?*
BARRY: Clint Eastwood.

Your own space _____

_____

_____

June 29

DINER: *Waiter, Waiter, do you call this a three-course meal?*
WAITER: Yes, sir. Two beans and a chip.

June 30

June's Loopy Limerick
There was a young man from Porthcawl
Who went to a fancy-dress ball.
His costume was great:
He went as a skate –
But the cat ate him up in the hall.

JULY

July 1

Keep on Knocking!
Knock, knock.
Who's there?
Little old lady.
Little old lady who?
I didn't know you could yodel.

Your own space _____
_____
_____

July 2

NEWSFLASH
A pint of milk and a tin of sardines were stolen from a supermarket early this morning. A police spokesman said that they were looking for a well-known cat burglar.

Your own space _____
_____
_____

July 3

Just a Thought

Firemen must be very popular people – wherever they go, they receive a warm welcome!

Your own space _____

_____

_____

July 4

Pun Fun:

How does an intruder get into your house?
Intruder window!

Your own space _____

_____

_____

July 5

SON: *You know something, Dad, I'm glad I wasn't born in Italy.*
FATHER: Why?
SON: *Well, I can't speak a word of Italian.*

Your own space _____

_____

_____

July 6

The American actor Sylvester Stallone was born on 6 July 1946. Perhaps you've seen him in *Rambo*, or one of the *Rocky* films where he plays a rags-to-riches boxer?

By the way, do you know what you get if you cross Sylvester Stallone with Frankenstein's monster? *The Rocky Horror Show!*

Your own space _____

_____

_____

July 7

Q. *What's the only sort of ring that's square?*
A. A boxing ring.

Your own space _____

_____

_____

July 8

Medical Advice
Avoid feeling run down – look both ways before crossing the road.

Your own space _____

_____

_____

July 9

Geography Lesson
How do you get two whales in a Volkswagen?
Over the Severn Bridge.

Your own space _____

_____

_____

July 10

Animal Quackers!
Why don't people who own cats ever shave?
Because eight out of ten owners said their cats prefer whiskers.

Your own space _____

_____

_____

July 11

A Shaggy Dog Story
Granny Ward had won a million pounds on the football pools, but as she was so old and frail her family were worried about telling her in case the excitement affected her heart. They called in the doctor to ask his advice. He offered to break the news gradually, and went up to the old lady's room, pretending he was on a regular visit.

After chatting of this and that, he remarked casually, 'Tell me, Mrs Ward, what would you do if you won a million pounds on the football pools?'

'Well,' said the old lady, 'that would be nice. I think, as you've always been so kind to me, I'd give half of it to you.'

As they sat anxiously downstairs, the family heard a sudden crash, as though someone had fallen heavily in Granny's room. They rushed up – to find the doctor had had a heart attack.

Your own space _____

_____

_____

July 12

Ancient Wisdom
You can lead a boy to water, but you can't make him wash his neck.

Your own space _____

_____

_____

July 13

Job Vacancy
Undertakers required. Must be prepared to take a stiff exam.

Your own space _____

_____

_____

July 14

Q. *How many 'D's are there in 'Match of the Day.'?*
A. Lots – (*Sing*) Dee Dee Dee Dee Dee Dee Dee Dee. . . .

Your own space _____

_____

_____

July 15

Potty People
What do you call a man with a seagull on his head?
Cliff!

Your own space _____

_____

_____

July 16

Here's a quick and simple practical joke to try on your parents.

You must include the word 'matterdear' in your conversation, as though it were some sort of exotic animal. Of course, it's really a made-up word designed to catch your parents out. The conversation might go like this:

'We had a very interesting geography lesson today. We learnt all about the mating habits of the matterdear.'

'What's a "matterdear"?'
'Nothing, Mum, I feel fine!'

Your own space _____

_____

_____

July 17

July's Loopy Limerick
A young man all bright and breezy
Said that eating mince pies was easy.
After downing fifteen,
His face went bright green,
And he looked and felt terribly queasy.

Your own space _____

_____

_____

July 18

One-liner of the Month.
My brother is such a bad athlete, he ran a bath the
other day and came second!

Your own space _____

_____

_____

July 19

DINER: *Waiter, Waiter, there's a fly in my soup.*
WAITER: Well, throw him a Polo – they make great
   rubber rings.

Your own space _____

_____

_____

July 20

Wise Saying of the Month
Television will never take the place of newspapers.
I mean, have you ever tried to swat a fly with a
television?

Your own space _____

_____

_____

July 21

Daft Definition
What's the definition of agony?
A centipede with bunions.

Your own space _____

_____

_____

July 22

Riddle-Tee-Hee!

Q. *Why did John Wayne take a hammer to bed with him?*
A. So he could hit the hay.

Your own space _____

_____

_____

July 23

ENGLISH TEACHER: *Why is there a hyphen in bird-cage?*
SILLY SARAH: For the bird to perch on, Miss.

Your own space _____

_____

_____

July 24

MAN: *I'd like to buy a dog.*
KENNEL OWNER: Certainly, Sir. What breed? A red
    setter, perhaps? Or a golden retriever?
MAN: *No, no, I don't want a coloured dog. Just a black and
    white one.*
KENNEL OWNER: Why is that?
MAN: *Isn't the licence cheaper?*

Your own space _____

_____

_____

July 25

Situation Vacant
BAKER REQUIRES ASSISTANT. NO ROOM
FOR LOAFERS.

Your own space _____

_____

_____

July 26

PATIENT: *Doctor, Doctor, I feel terrible. People keep
mistaking me for a dog.*
DOCTOR: Well, I must say your nose does feel a little
dry.

Your own space _____

_____

_____

July 27

Idiot Corner
My brother is so silly – when a woman came to the
door saying that she was collecting for the local Old
People's Home, he didn't give her money, he gave
her Granny!

Your own space _____

_____

_____

July 28

Notice in shop window
Harry Harris butchers pigs like his father.

Your own space _____

_____

_____

July 29

A great new book has just come out for all lovers of
astrology. It's called *What Sign are You?* by Horace
Scopes.

Your own space _____

_____

_____

July 30

CYNTHIA: *My dad was cutting up the Brussels sprouts for
lunch on Sunday, when the knife slipped and stabbed him
in the heart.*
TRACY: Blimey! What did your mum do?
CYNTHIA: *She opened up a tin of carrots.*

Your own space _____

_____

_____

July 31

Let's finish off the month with a tantalizing tongue-twister

Goodie Twoshoes' two shoes got so grubby that Goodie Twoshoes took her two shoes to the Grand Old Goodie Shoeshine's shoe shop.

Your own space _____

_____

_____

AUGUST

August 1

Daft Definition

What does 'important' mean?
A foreign insect.

Your own space _____

_____

_____

August 2

Medical Madness

PATIENT: *Doctor, Doctor, I keep thinking I'm London Bridge.*
DOCTOR: My dear man, what's come over you?

Your own space _____

_____

_____

August 3

A Shaggy Knock-knock Story!
Knock, knock.
Who's there?
Uncle.
Uncle who?
Uncle Arthur.

Knock, knock.
Who's there?
Uncle.
Uncle who?
Uncle Arthur.

Knock, knock.
Who's there?
Auntie.
Auntie who?
Auntie glad it's not Uncle Arthur!

Your own space _____

_____

_____

August 4

Just a Thought
When the wheel was first invented, did it cause a
revolution?

Your own space _____

_____

_____

August 5

1ST DOG: *What's your name?*
2ND DOG: I'm not sure but I think it's Down Boy.

Your own space _____

_____

_____

August 6

LAWYER: *It didn't take long to wind up Mr Graham's estate after he died.*
ACCOUNTANT: Why was that?
LAWYER: *All he left was a grandfather clock.*

Your own space _____

_____

_____

August 7

MARY: *Our PE mistress says that exercise is so good for you it can solve all your problems.*
MAUREEN: I know. No matter what is wrong, she says that gym'll fix it.

Your own space _____

_____

_____

August 8

Q. *How do you get an elephant in a matchbox?*
A. Take the matches out first.

Your own space _____

_____

_____

August 9

LADY CRABTREE: *Jeeves, there is a mouse in the blue drawing-room.*
JEEVES: Very good, Madam. I'll ascertain whether the cat is at home.

Your own space _____

_____

_____

August 10

MR WILLIAMS: *I went on holiday last week, and found out why they're called five-star hotels.*
MR EASTON: Why?
MR WILLIAMS: *Because they charge such astronomical prices.*

Your own space _____

_____

_____

August 11

A Cheeky Challenge

Do you know anyone who drives a car? If you do, test their knowledge of the elementary Highway Code with this Cheeky Challenge.

Ask them to spell these words:

Top (T-O-P)
Drop (D-R-O-P)
Shop (S-H-O-P)
Mop (M-O-P)

Then quickly ask them what you should do when the traffic lights turn green. You'll be surprised how many drivers will get it wrong and say STOP!

Your own space _____

_____

_____

August 12

Q. *What did the tablecloth say to the table?*
A. Don't move, I've got you covered.

Your own space _____

_____

_____

August 13

Hey Diddle Diddle, Here Comes a Riddle

Q. *What do you call a hippy's wife?*
A. Mississippi!

Your own space _____

_____

_____

August 14

August's Mighty Mouthful
Oswald Whittle's whistle outwhistles all other whistler's whistles in Oswaldtwistle.

Your own space _____

_____

August 15

Potty People
What do you call a man with a car on his head?
Jack!

Your own space _____

_____

_____

August 16

At Cross Purposes!
What do you get if you cross a fish with a couple of suitcases?
Swimming trunks.

Your own space _____

_____

August 17

Our dog thinks it's a chicken. We'd like to take it to the vet, but we need the eggs!

Your own space _____

_____

_____

August 18

NEWSFLASH

Thieves broke into a hairdressers' shop this morning, stealing £5000 worth of goods before making a quick getaway. Police think they may have taken a short cut when leaving the shop.

Your own space _____

_____

_____

August 19

One-liner of the Month

Children really brighten up a home – they never turn any lights off!

Your own space _____

_____

_____

August 20

Did you hear about the hyena who swallowed an Oxo cube?
He made a real laughing stock of himself!

Your own space _____

_____

_____

August 21

Musical Knowledge
What sort of trousers do piano players wear?
Cords.

Your own space _____

_____

_____

August 22

At last a book that will please everybody!
All Your Problems solved by Alex Plain.

Your own space _____

_____

_____

August 23

Notice in restaurant window
Dinner will be served from 6.30 until the end of
summer.

_____

_____

August 24

August's Loopy Limerick
There was a young feller from Poole,
Who'd not once in his life been to school.
His parents had tried,
But he'd always replied:
'No school – that's my number one rule!'

_____

_____

August 25

Service Not Included!
CUSTOMER: *Does the band play requests?*
WAITER: Certainly, Sir.
CUSTOMER: *Then ask them to play cards until I've finished my meal.*

_____

_____

August 26

What was the tortoise doing on the motorway?
About one metre an hour.

Your own space _____

_____

_____

August 27

Food for Thought!
If a couple of Irish potatoes went on holiday to
France, would they come back as French Fries?

Your own space _____

_____

_____

August 28

Keep on Knocking!
Knock, knock.
Who's there?
House.
House who?
Hugh's fine. How's Clive?

Your own space _____

_____

_____

August 29

The wonderful Michael Jackson was born on 29 August 1958. It's amazing to think that his 'Thriller' album is the best-selling LP record of all time.
Do you know what sort of umbrella Michael Jackson carries when it's raining?
A wet one!

Your own space _____

_____

_____

August 30

NEWS . . . NEWS . . . NEWS
'Two hundred dairy cows slipped and fell over today as they were herded along an icy country lane. A spokesperson for the Farmers' Association said that the incident was unfortunate, but added that it was no use crying over spilt milk.'

Your own space _____

_____

_____

August 31

TEACHER: *Which poet wrote 'To a Nightingale'?*
DANNY: Whoever it was, I bet he didn't get a reply!

Your own space _____

_____

_____

SEPTEMBER

September 1

Advertisement in the *Morning Herald*
Vacancy for rubbish-collector. No training given.
You will pick it up as you go along.

Your own space _____

_____

_____

September 2

1ST MAN: *I bought a second-hand jumper yesterday. It was only 10p, even though it was in mint condition.*
2ND MAN: Why was it so cheap?
1ST MAN: *It had a hole in the middle!*

Your own space _____

_____

_____

September 3

Have you heard about the farmer who ploughed his field with a steam roller so that he could grow mashed potatoes?

Your own space _____

_____

_____

September 4

Someone at the Door?
Knock, knock.
Who's there?
Butcher.
Butcher who?
Butcher left leg in, butcher left leg out, in, out, in out. . .

Your own space _____

_____

_____

September 5

Riddle-Tee-Hee
Q. *What's the opposite of a restaurant?*
A. A workeraunt!

Your own space _____

_____

_____

September 6

Potty People
What do you call a man with a vaulting horse on his head?
Jim!

Your own space ―――――――――――――――

―――――――――――――――――――――――

September 7

Today is National Sombrero Day in Mexico, the day
when all Mexicans throw their sombrero hats into
the air as the clock strikes twelve.
Do you know who Mexico's most famous fat man is?
Pauncho Villa, of course.

Your own space ―――――――――――――――

―――――――――――――――――――――――

September 8

Just a Thought
Did the missionaries of the nineteenth century give
the cannibals their first taste of Christianity?

Your own space ―――――――――――――――

―――――――――――――――――――――――

September 9

Crazy Graffiti
I've half a mind to go to that meeting on
'Schizophrenia' tonight.

Your own space _____

_____

_____

September 10

NEWS ... NEWS ... NEWS
'British Telecom have decided not to make telephone
poles any longer. A spokesman says that in their
opinion they are quite long enough already.'

Your own space _____

_____

_____

September 11

COOKERY TEACHER: *How can we prevent food from going
    bad?*
SUSIE: By eating it, Miss.

Your own space _____

_____

_____

September 12

One-liner of the Month
The only thing I grow in my garden is tired.

Your own space _____

_____

_____

September 13

Why not get this rather painful book out of the
library:
Six of the Best by Major B Hindsaw

Your own space _____

_____

_____

September 14

**Try this simple practical joke on your friends
today**.
Tell them you can stay under water for ten minutes.
They won't believe you, but this is how it is done.
Simply fill a glass or a cup with water and hold it over
your head. You can then stay under water for as long
as you like! (Be careful to use the right words,
though, don't say you can hold your breath under
water for ten minutes or you'll lose the bet!)

Your own space _____

_____

_____

September 15

It's a Crazy World!
Why is it that in the newspapers, people always seem to die in alphabetical order?

Your own space _____

_____

_____

September 16

What does a short-sighted frog do?
Goes to the hoptician.

Your own space _____

_____

_____

September 17

Q. What do the Red Indians call a giggle?
A. A Minihaha!

Your own space _____

_____

_____

September 18

Daft Definition
What's an eclipse?
It's what a hairdresser does!

September 19

The lovely Sixties model Twiggy was born on 19
September 1949. Do you know what her rather
overweight older sister was called?
That's right – Branchy!

September 20

September's Mighty Mouthful
Esther Harris the elderly heiress could not hear with
either ear.

September 21

Q. *Why are dentists such dull party guests?*
A. Because they're always boring.

September 22

Medical Madness

PATIENT: *Doctor, Doctor, my hair's started to fall out. Can you give me anything to keep it in?*

DOCTOR: Certainly, take this shoebox.

Your own space _____

_____

_____

September 23

September's Loopy Limerick

There was an old woman from Clyde,
Who ate fifty apples and died.
The apples fermented
Inside the lamented
And made cider inside 'er inside.

Your own space _____

_____

_____

September 24

BIOLOGY TEACHER: *What kind of birds do we usually find in captivity?*

SIMON: Jail-birds, Sir.

Your own space _____

_____

_____

September 25

'When I was in China,' said the tourist, 'I saw a woman hanging from a tree.'
'Shanghai?'
'No, only about one metre from the ground.'

Your own space _____

_____

_____

September 26

Hey Diddle Diddle, Here comes a Riddle!
Q. *What do goblins make cakes with?*
A. Elf-raising flour.

Your own space _____

_____

_____

September 27

BOSS: *What's your name?*
NEW BOY: 'Arold 'Iggins.
BOSS: *Say 'Sir' when you speak to me.*
NEW BOY: All right, then, Sir 'Arold 'Iggins.

Your own space _____

_____

_____

September 28

My cousin's just got a job as a waiter at a top London hotel. He's called Roland Butter!

Your own space _____

_____

_____

September 29

Wise Saying of the Month
No painter is so bad he can't draw breath.

Your own space _Richards birthday_

_____

_____

September 30

What do you have to know to be an auctioneer?
Lots.

Your own space _____

_____

_____

OCTOBER

October 1

Down at the Doctor's

PATIENT: *Doctor, Doctor, I think I've got measles.*
DOCTOR: Now, let's not be rash. . . .

Your own space _____

_____

_____

October 2

MUM: *Why are you crying?*
SALLY: I hurt my finger.
MUM: *When did you do that?*
SALLY: Half an hour ago.
MUM: *I didn't hear you crying then.*
SALLY: No, I thought you were out.

Your own space _____

_____

_____

October 3

Sightseeing
If you stand on top of the Eiffel Tower, what's the most distant object you can see?
The sun.

Your own space _____

_____

_____

October 4

Just a Thought
Do tramps cover themselves with newspapers at night in order to dress with *The Times*?

Your own space _____

_____

_____

October 5

For Better Or Verse
Hickory dickory dock,
Three mice ran up the clock.
The clock struck one,
But the other two managed to escape!

Your own space _____

_____

_____

October 6

One-liner of the Month
My wife's just had plastic surgery – they cut up all her credit cards!

Your own space _____

_____

_____

October 7

NEWS ... NEWS ... NEWS
A cure has just been invented for water on the knee.
A tap on the leg.

Your own space _____

_____

_____

October 8

Keep on knocking!
Knock, knock.
Who's there?
Andy.
Andy who?
Andy things these door-knockers.

Your own space _____

_____

_____

October 9

KEITH: *I've decided to buy a skunk and keep it in my room as a pet.*

MOTHER: But what about the horrible smell?

KEITH: *The skunk will just have to get used to it.*

Your own space _____

_____

_____

October 10

October's Mighty Mouthful

Can you construct coal carts out of cardboard crates? If you can construct coal carts out of cardboard crates, people will be compelled to call you clever clogs!

Your own space _____

_____

_____

October 11

SAMMY: *I'd like to get a job as a puppeteer.*

CAREERS OFFICER: Do you know anyone in the business who can pull a few strings?

Your own space _____

_____

_____

October 12

More Potty People
What do you call a man with a swag bag over his shoulder?
Rob!

Your own space _____

_____

_____

October 13

October's Loopy Limerick
There was a footballer called Claude
Who during a game became bored.
With the score at two all
He picked up the ball,
Dribbled round his own goalie and scored.

Your own space _____

_____

_____

October 14

Sign in florist's window
Helper for flower shop wanted. Budding geniuses
preferred.

Your own space _____

_____

_____

October 15

Why is money called dough?
Because everybody kneads it.

Your own space _____

_____

_____

October 16

Film Facts
What were Lassie's last words?
Well, I'll be doggone!

Your own space _____

_____

_____

October 17

Ancient Wisdom
Don't expect sunshine if the weatherman is wearing an overcoat.

Your own space _____

_____

_____

October 18

Riddle-Tee-Hee!
Q. *What do bees say when the sun's out?*
A. 'Swarm!'

Your own space _____

_____

_____

October 19

Daft Definition
What's a myth?
An unmarried woman with a lisp!

Your own space _____

_____

_____

October 20

How many ears has Mr Spock got?
A right ear, a left ear, and a final frontier.

Your own space _____

_____

_____

October 21

Crazy Graffiti
They don't make cars like they auto.

Your own space _____

_____

_____

October 22

Cheeky Challenge

Bet a friend you can push yourself through the keyhole of a door. Your friend won't believe you – but this is how it is done. Simply write the word 'myself' on a piece of paper and push it through the keyhole. You will have pushed yourself through the hole as you said you would!

Your own space _____

_____

_____

October 23

Medical Madness

PATIENT: *Doctor, Doctor, I keep thinking I'm a goat.*
DOCTOR: How long have you been feeling like this?
PATIENT: *Ever since I was a kid.*

Your own space _____

_____

_____

October 24

PASSER-BY: *Is this river good for fish?*
FISHERMAN: It must be. I can't get any of them to leave it.

Your own space _____

_____

_____

October 25

Old Proverb
When the cat's away, the house smells better!

Your own space _____

_____

_____

October 26

NEWSFLASH
If anyone has any information concerning the
whereabouts of the rare birds which escaped from
the zoo last week, would they please contact the
Flying Squad immediately.

Your own space _____

_____

_____

October 27

Jimmy came clattering down the stairs very loudly,
much to his father's annoyance. He was sent back
upstairs and told to come down again quietly.

    There was a silence, then Jimmy reappeared in the
front room. 'That's better,' said his father. 'Why
don't you always come down like that?'

    'Suits me,' said Jimmy. 'I slid down the banisters.'

Your own space _____

_____

_____

October 28

Hey Diddle Diddle, Here Comes a Riddle!

Q. *Where was Solomon's temple?*
A. On the side of his head.

Your own space _____

_____

October 29

What do robbers have for dinner?
Beefburglars.

Your own space _____

_____

October 30

What lies on the ground 100 feet up in the air?
A centipede on its back.

Your own space _____

_____

October 31

A Hallowe'en Howler!

How does a ghost begin a letter?
Tomb it may concern.

Your own space _____

_____

NOVEMBER

November 1

Let's start November with a Ridiculous Riddle!

Q.   *What do you get if you give beaten egg-whites and sugar to a monkey?*

A.   Meringue utan.

Your own space _____

_____

_____

November 2

Can you get your tongue around this Terrible Twister?

SILVER THIMBLES

(You may think it's easy, but just try saying it quickly five times in succession.)

Your own space _____

_____

_____

November 3

Geography Lesson
What's the friendliest state in America?
Ohio!

Your own space _____

_____

_____

November 4

Recipe Corner
Do you know how to make Shepherd's Pie?
Well, first you've got to catch a shepherd, then . . .

Your own space _____

_____

_____

November 5

Knock, knock.
Who's there?
Guy.
Guy who?
Guy Fawkes, because today is Guy Fawkes' Day!

Your own space _____

_____

_____

November 6

CUSTOMER: *Have you got anything to cure fleas on a dog?*
PET SHOP OWNER: I don't know, what's wrong with
   the fleas?

Your own space _____

_____

_____

November 7

Ancient Wisdom
It doesn't matter which side your bread is buttered
on – eat both sides!

Your own space _____

_____

_____

November 8

Keep on Knocking!
Knock, knock.
Who's there?
William.
William who?
William mind your own business!

Your own space _____

_____

_____

November 9

Daft Definition

What's a pauper?
The guy who married mamma!

Your own space _____

_____

_____

November 10

SAY IT WITH FLOWERS – Hit someone over the
head with a bunch of daffodils!

Your own space _____

_____

_____

November 11

Hey Diddle Diddle, Here comes a Riddle!

Q.   *Why are N and O the most important letters in the
     alphabet?*
A.   Because you can't get ON without them.

Your own space _____

_____

_____

November 12

One-liner of the Month
He's such a bad boxer the crowd call him Picasso –
because he's always on the canvas!

Your own space _____

_____

_____

November 13

MRS KING: *Our cat can play chess, you know.*
MRS WEST: Really? It must be very clever.
MRS KING: *I suppose so – but I'm still three-two up in games!*

Your own space _____

_____

_____

November 14

JENNY: *Dad, have you got any holes in your underpants?*
DAD: Certainly not.
JENNY: *Then how do you get them over your feet?*

Your own space _____

_____

_____

November 15

Q. *How does a witch tell the time?*
A. With her witch watch.

Your own space _____

_____

_____

November 16

Why did the policeman start crying?
Because he wasn't allowed to take his panda to bed with him!

Your own space _____

_____

_____

November 17

GEORGE: *Alcohol was the cause of my father's death.*
HARRY: You mean he drank too much?
GEORGE: *No. A case of wine fell on his head.*

Your own space _____

_____

_____

November 18

Why are waiters such optimists?
Because they believe that money grows on trays!

Your own space _____

_____

_____

November 19

Medical Madness

PATIENT: *Doctor, Doctor, I keep thinking I'm a pack of cards.*

DOCTOR: Not now, Mr Jones. I'll deal with you later.

Your own space _____

_____

_____

November 20

Just a Thought
If ants are such busy insects, why is it that they always find time to turn up at picnics?

Your own space _____

_____

_____

November 21

NEWS . . . NEWS . . . NEWS
'A car crashed into a tree on the A1 earlier today. The driver, a tree surgeon by profession, had to be treated for shock when he found out that he'd hit one of his own patients.'

Your own space _____

_____

_____

November 22

November's Top Three Titles
The Great Escape   by Wendy Leave
Fruit Machines   by Noah Chance
The Human Body   by Anna Tomical

Your own space _____

_____

_____

November 23

Animal Quackers!
What's a frog's favourite sweet?
A lollihop!

Your own space _____

_____

_____

November 24

The Return of the Potty People
What do you call a man with six rabbits on his head?
Warren!

Your own space _____

_____

_____

November 25

1ST MAN: *What do you regard as the height of stupidity?*
2ND MAN: How tall are you?

Your own space _____

_____

_____

November 26

Wise Saying of the Month
Cleanliness is next to impossible.

Your own space _____

_____

_____

November 27

You can't win!
Eric was given two apples, a big one and a little one,
by his mum, and told to share them with his sister,
Betty. He gave the small one to Betty and ate the big
one himself.

'That's not fair,' said Betty. 'If Mum had given
them to me I'd have given you the big one and kept
the small one for myself.'

Your own space _____

_____

_____

November 28

Q. *Why do bears have fur coats?*
A. Because they would look rather stupid in plastic macs!

Your own space _____

_____

_____

November 29

Advertisement in paper
Publican required. Must have spent at least ten years behind bars.

Your own space _____

_____

_____

November 30

Here's a Loopy Limerick for St Andrew's Day!
There was a Scots lady called Sue
Who spent all her time on the loo.
She said: 'All I lack is
A plateful of haggis.
Can you do that? Och aye the noo!'

Your own space _____

_____

_____

DECEMBER

December 1

Let's start this Christmas month with another Ridiculous Riddle!

Q.   *How did Shakespeare manage to write so many plays?*
A.   Because where there's a Will, there's a way.

Your own space _____

_____

_____

December 2

Just a Thought
If you think about it, Robin Hood was very sensible when he decided to rob the rich. I mean, he wouldn't have got much money by robbing the poor!

Your own space _____

_____

_____

December 3

Do you know anyone who's in love? If you do, here's the perfect Christmas present – a new book called *Yuletide Romance* by Miss L. Tow.

Your own space _____

_____

_____

December 4

Have you heard the joke about the ten metre high wall? On second thoughts, I'd better not tell it to you. You might never get over it.

Your own space _____

_____

_____

December 5

OLD WOMAN: *Could you see me across this busy road, Sonny?*
BOY SCOUT: Of course. My eyesight's not that bad, you know!

Your own space _____

_____

_____

December 6

Today is National Goldfish Day in Patagonia. Which reminds me of a very fishy story:

FATHER: *Have you changed the goldfish water this week?*
SON: No, they haven't drunk what I gave them last week yet.

Your own space ———————— ~~ins birthday~~

—————————————————————

—————————————————————

December 7

Doctor's Advice
If you have trouble sleeping at night, don't worry, there's a simple solution. Just move towards the edge of your bed, and you'll soon drop off.

Your own space ————————————

—————————————————————

—————————————————————

December 8

Crazy Graffiti
My parents made me a punk rocker!
(*Underneath which is written:*)
If I gave them some wool, would they make one for me too?

Your own space ————————————

—————————————————————

—————————————————————

December 9

What do bees do if they want to use public transport?
Wait at a buzz stop.

Your own space _Kevins birtday_

December 10

Potty People
What do you call a girl with a bucket and spade on her head?
Sandy!

Your own space _____

December 11

GARETH: *My dad's just got a new job with 300 people under him.*
BOBBY: Gosh, he must be very important.
GARETH: *No, he's just the gardener at the local cemetery.*

Your own space _____

December 12

One-liner of the Month
Robots don't have brothers, they just have tran*sisters*.

Your own space _____

_____

_____

December 13

Ad. in *The Western Advertiser*
Are you in a hurry to pass your driving test? Come to the Sure School of Motoring – crash courses available.

Your own space _____

_____

_____

December 14

LADY: *I'd like to buy a fur coat, please.*
SHOP ASSISTANT: Certainly, Madam, what fur exactly?
LADY: *To keep me warm, you fool.*

Your own space _____

_____

_____

December 15

Medical Madness
PATIENT: *Doctor, Doctor, my husband's been a bundle of nerves ever since he won the Pools last week.*

DOCTOR: Don't worry, Madam, I think I can relieve him of that.

Your own space _____

_____

_____

December 16

Wise Saying of the Month
Early to bed and early to rise means you never see any of your friends.

Your own space _____

_____

_____

December 17

December's Loopy Limerick
There was a young fella called Clive,
Who spent most of his time in a hive.
From his head to his knees
He was covered in bees –
It's a wonder that Clive's still alive!

Your own space _____

_____

_____

December 18

Steven Spielberg, the man responsible for such great films as *Jaws* and *E.T.*, was born on 18 December 1947.

My favourite film of recent years is all about cricket. Maybe you've seen it – it's called *The Umpire Strikes Back!*

Your own space _____

_____

_____

December 19

Q. *Where did the vicar's wife go when her husband disappeared?*
A. The Missing Parsons Bureau!

Your own space _____

_____

_____

December 20

Quick Quip!
The problem with cannibal jokes is that they're in very bad taste.

Your own space _____

_____

_____

December 21

SUE: *My elder brother is a stand-up comedian.*
TRACY: Really, what's his name?
SUE: *Jess Joe King.*

Your own space _____

_____

_____

December 22

Hey Diddle Diddle, Here Comes a Riddle!

Q. *Where do cows go to be entertained?*
A. The mooooovies.

Your own space _Mums   birthday_

_____

_____

December 23

A Tricky Tongue-twister
THREE THRICE-FREED THIEVES
(It may be short, but it's very difficult!)

Your own space _____

_____

_____

December 24

A Christmas Eve Thought
Central heating has got a lot to answer for at
Christmas. I mean, how is Santa Claus expected to
slide down a radiator?

Your own space _____

_____

_____

December 25

It's Christmas Day!
Do you know what Father Christmas's wife is called?
Mary Christmas.

Your own space _____

_____

_____

December 26

Christmas is a time when you need a lot of get-up-
and-go. Unfortunately, by the time Boxing Day
arrives, most people's get-up-and-go has already got
up and gone!

Your own space _____

_____

_____

December 27

1ST GIRL: *Next year my mother has decided to cross the turkey with an octopus.*
2ND GIRL: Why's that?
1ST GIRL: *Because with the number of people in our family, it's the only way we can all have a leg each.*

Your own space _____

_____

_____

December 28

Notice in Job Centre
Additional staff wanted at the Blotto Blotting Paper Company. Apply now if you enjoy really absorbing work.

Your own space _____

_____

_____

December 29

The Return of the Potty People
What do you call a man with an electric plug coming out of his head?
Mike!

Your own space _____

_____

_____

December 30

Holy Cow!
Why was Samson the most popular character in the Bible?
Because he brought the house down!

Your own space _____

_____

_____

December 31

December's Knock-knock
Knock, knock.
Who's there?
Juno.
Juno who?
Juno what day it is — New Year's Eve, of course!

Your own space _____

_____

_____

JOKE BOOKS

If you're an eager Beaver reader, perhaps you ought to try some more of our hilarious Beaver joke books. They are available in bookshops or they can be ordered directly from us. Just complete the form below and enclose the right amount of money and the books will be sent to you at home.

☐	THE BROWNIE JOKE BOOK	Brownies	95p
☐	MORE BROWNIE JOKES	Brownies	95p
☐	JELLYBONE GRAFFITI BOOK	Therese Birch	95p
☐	SCHOOL GRAFFITI	Peter Eldin	95p
☐	SKOOL FOR LAUGHS	Peter Eldin	95p
☐	THE WOOLLY JUMPER JOKE BOOK	Peter Eldin	95p
☐	THE FUNNIEST JOKE BOOK	Jim Eldridge	£1.00
☐	THE WOBBLY JELLY JOKE BOOK	Jim Eldridge	95p
☐	HOW TO HANDLE GROWN-UPS	Jim Eldridge	£1.00
☐	THE CRAZY JOKER'S HANDBOOK	Janet Rogers	£1.00
☐	THE CRAZY JOKE BOOK STRIKES BACK	Janet Rogers	£1.00
☐	THE ELEPHANT JOKE BOOK	Katie Wales	£1.00
☐	FALL ABOUT WITH FLO	Floella Benjamin	£1.25

And if you would like to hear more about Beaver Books, and find out all the latest news, don't forget the BEAVER BULLETIN. Just send a stamped, self-addressed envelope to Beaver Books, 62 – 65 Chandos Place, Covent Garden, London WC2N 4NW.

If you would like to order books, please send this form, and the money due to:

HAMLYN PAPERBACK CASH SALES, PO BOX 11, FALMOUTH, CORNWALL TR10 9EN.

Send a cheque or postal order, and don't forget to include postage at the following rates: UK: 55p for first book, 22p for the second, 14p thereafter; BFPO and Eire: 55p for first book, 22p for the second, 14p per copy for next 7 books, 8p per book thereafter; Overseas £1.00 for first book, 25p thereafter.

NAME..

ADDRESS...

....

Please print clearly